SPAIN

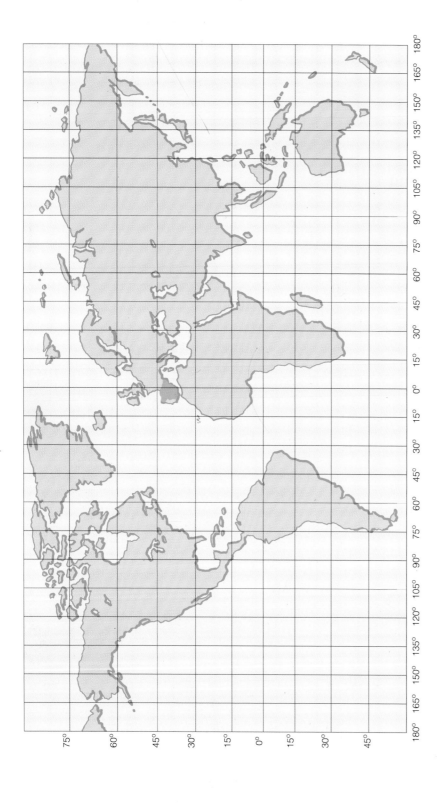

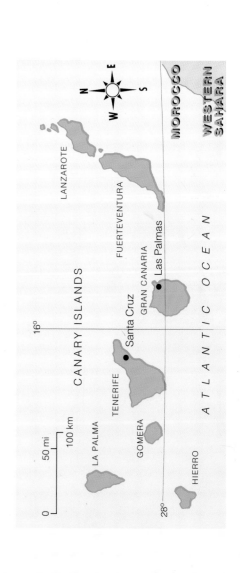

CANARY ISLANDS

LANZAROTE

FUERTEVENTURA

GRAN CANARIA

Las Palmas

TENERIFE

Santa Cruz

LA PALMA

GOMERA

HIERRO

ATLANTIC OCEAN

MOROCCO

WESTERN SAHARA

16°

28°

0

50 mi

100 km

N
W   E
S

SPAIN

Anna Selby

RAINTREE STECK-VAUGHN
PUBLISHERS

Austin, Texas

Published by Raintree Steck-Vaughn Publishers, an imprint of
Steck-Vaughn Company

Design	Roger Kohn
Editors	Diana Russell, Helene Resky
DTP editor	Helen Swansbourne
Picture research	Valerie Mulcahy
Illustration	János Márffy
	Coral Mula
Consultant	David Barrs
Commissioning editor	Debbie Fox

We are grateful to the following for permission
to reproduce photographs:
Front Cover: Sefton Photo Library/TRIP *above*, Magnum
(B. Barbey) *below;* AGE Fotostock, pages 10, 16 *below*,
18 *below*, 20, 24 *below*; Allsport, page 9; The Casement
Collection/TRIP, pages 8–9, 12 *below*, 13; Bruce Coleman,
page 39 *above* and *below*; Adolfo Dominguez, page 41 *above*
(Otoño Invierno); Eye Ubiquitous/TRIP, pages 32 *above*,
35 *below*; Tim Graham, page 28; Robert Harding Picture
Library, pages 11, 23; The Image Bank, pages 24 *above*, 25,
27 *above*, 40–41; Anthony King, pages 12 *above*, 21, 37;
Life File/TRIP, pages 17, 18 *above*, 27 *below*, 30, 31, 32
below, 35 *above*; John Edward Linden/TRIP, page 42;
Magnum, pages 22 (Stuart Franklin), 34 and 36 (Fred Mayer);
Network Photographers, page 29 (C. Pillitz); Picturepoint,
pages 16 *above*, 26, 33, 38, 43; Helene Rogers/TRIP,
page 14; Spanish National Tourist Office, page 15.

The statistics given in this book are the most up to date
available at the time of going to press

Library of Congress Cataloging-in-Publication Data
Selby, Anna.
Spain / Anna Selby.
p. cm. — (Country fact files)
Includes index.
ISBN 0-8114-1848-0
1. Spain – Juvenile literature. [1. Spain.]
I. Title. II. Series.
DP17.S39 1993
946–dc20
93-28438
CIP AC

Printed and bound in Hong Kong by
Paramount Printing Group Ltd

1 2 3 4 5 6 7 8 9 0 HK 99 98 97 96 95 94

Words that are explained in the glossary are printed in
SMALL CAPITALS the first time they are mentioned in the text.

C O N T E N T S

INTRODUCTION

Spain is the second-largest country in Europe. Many non-Spanish people have spent their vacations on the Spanish coast or on Spanish islands — the Canaries or the Balearics. However, Spain has only recently been so open to visitors. For more than 30 years, it was cut off from the rest of the world under the DICTATORSHIP of General Franco (1939–1975). During that time, laws were very strict, and people were not allowed to criticize the government in any way. At the end of his life, General Franco brought back the monarchy, and now King Juan Carlos is the head of a democratic monarchy. Spain did not join the European Community (EC) until 1986, but it is now eager to be part of Europe.

Although it is becoming increasingly industrialized, much of rural Spain is still quite poor. Many people are moving from the country to the cities or the coast, where there is a thriving tourist industry. But farming is still important, and Spain is famous for many of its crops, such as olives and oranges, which can only grow in such a warm climate.

Religion still has a very big influence on most Spanish people, who are almost all Roman Catholics. Spain's traditional way of life is strong, too, as can be seen from such popular sports as bullfighting and the Basque game of PELOTA. There are strong regional identities, like that of Andalusia in the south, with its flamenco dancing and its food with Moorish (North African) influences.

As Spain catches up with other industrialized countries, new problems are emerging, such as pollution from cars in cities and the destruction of some beautiful coastline by tourist developments.

▲ *Although some of Spain's agriculture is becoming more mechanized, there are many areas where the land is tilled in the traditional way, using a plow pulled by oxen. This farmer is typical of many in the south, where the old methods are common.*

▶ *In 1992 Barcelona hosted the Olympic Games. This picture shows the spectacular closing ceremony.*

SPAIN AT A GLANCE

- Area: 194,896 square miles (504,748 sq km)
- Population: 39 million
- Density: 202 people per square mile (77.9 people per sq km)
- Capital: Madrid, population 4,500,000
- Other main cities: Barcelona 1,800,000; Valencia 800,000; Seville 700,000; Saragossa 600,000
- Language: Spanish (Castilian)
- Religion: Roman Catholic
- Currency: pesetas, written as ptas
- Economy: traditionally farming, now industrializing
- Major resources: climate
- Major products: olive oil, wines, tourist goods, leather, iron, and steel
- Environmental problems: DEFORESTATION, DESERTIFICATION, pollution

THE LANDSCAPE

Spain forms the main part of the Iberian Peninsula, which it shares with Portugal. It is the second most mountainous country in Europe, after Switzerland. Much of Spain is very different from the country that tourists visit.

In the north is "Green Spain," which includes the Basque country, Cantabria, Asturias, and Galicia. This area hugs the northern and western coasts of Spain facing the Atlantic Ocean. The large, rocky inlets here are known as RIAS. Northern Spain as a whole is quite wild and mountainous and very sparsely populated. The famous Picos de Europa ("Peaks of Europe") in Asturias reach 8,586 feet (2,615 m) and form part of the Cantabrian Mountains, where the Ebro River rises.

▲ *In the center of Spain is Las Bardeñas desert of Navarra, with its strangely sculpted landscape.*

MIÑO RIVER
PICOS DE EUROPA
CANTABRIAN MOUNTAINS
PYRENEES
Pico de Aneto
11,176 ft (3,404 m)
Duero River
Ebro River
Jalón River
COSTA BRAVA
M E S E T A
N
Tagus River
Záncara River
BALEARIC ISLANDS
Guadiana River
0   50 mi
100 km
Guadalquivir River
COSTA BLANCA
DOÑANA NATIONAL PARK
SIERRA NEVADA
△11,433 ft
Mulhacén (3,482 m)
CANARY ISLANDS
Pico de Teide
12,207 ft (3,718 m)
COSTA DEL SOL

KEY FACTS

● Approximately 124,000 square miles (200,000 sq km), or 40 percent, of Spain is covered by a central PLATEAU called the MESETA, 1,642 feet (500 m) high.

● Madrid is the highest European capital, 2,190 feet (667 m) above sea level.

● Spain has only 7 navigable rivers, none of which is near Madrid.

● The longest river is the Ebro at 564 miles (910 km).

▲ *The Pyrenees, which rise to more than 9,850 feet (3,000 m), are the mountains in the northeast of Spain that form a natural border with France. There are heavy snowfalls in winter, and the buildings have steep-sided roofs so that the snow will slide off instead of building up on top of them.*

The Ebro River is Spain's longest river at 564 miles (910 km). It is the only Spanish river that flows into the Mediterranean. All the others flow into the Atlantic.

Spain's mountain areas are riddled with naturally-formed caves (there are approximately 10,000). One of the most famous is at Altamira in Cantabria, which is 887 feet (270 m) long. Its walls are covered with rock paintings dating from 13,000 B.C.

The east coast of Spain faces the Mediterranean. This area includes the regions of Catalonia, Valencia, and Murcia. Northern Catalonia is dominated by the Pyrenees, which extend westward into Navarra and form Spain's border with France. The highest point at 11,176 feet (3,404 m) is Pico de Aneto. Catalonia's coastline includes the Costa Brava with its rocky cliffs and small sandy coves, some of which have been destroyed by tourism.

South of Catalonia are Valencia and Murcia, with the long white beaches of the Costa Blanca. Southwest of Murcia is Andalusia, home to both the white sandy beaches of the Costa del Sol and the mountains of the SIERRA Nevada ("snowy mountains"), the highest mountains on mainland Spain at almost 11,433 feet (3,500 m).

KEY FACTS

● Spain has 4,886 miles (7,880 km) of coastline, of which 24 percent is beach.
● The last volcano to erupt in Spain was in La Palma in the Canary Islands in 1971.
● Spain's highest mountain, Pico de Teide, is 12,207 feet (3,718 m) and is located in Tenerife.
● The Canary Islands are nearer to Africa, which is 71 miles (115 km) away , than they are to Spain.

▶ *Benidorm is one of the most popular tourist destinations because of its white, sandy beaches and long, hot, sunny summers.*

The Picos de Europa in the north of Spain are wild, the home of many rare animals and birds. Because the weather is very wet here, it is green and lush.

Like all of the Canary Islands, Lanzarote was formed by a volcanic eruption. It is dry and barren, like the deserts of North Africa.

Opposite the coast of Andalusia is Gibraltar, a limestone island only 3 miles (5 km) long and 1.3 miles (2 km) wide, rising to a height of 121 feet (426 m) and linked to the mainland by a narrow ISTHMUS. It is the cause of a long-standing disagreement between Spain and Great Britain, and it is still British territory.

Much of inland Spain is covered by a high central plateau known as the Meseta ("little table"). In this area is the old kingdom of Castile, now divided into Castile-Leon and Castile-La Mancha, famous as the setting of Cervantes' novel *Don Quixote*. It is an area of vast plains, broken by occasional rocky outcrops, such as the stunning gorge of Cuenca with its "hanging houses" that have been built right at the edge of a precipice. Also within inland Spain are Aragon and Navarra, extending southward from the foothills of the Pyrenees, an area of spectacular mountainous countryside.

There are two sets of Spanish islands — the five Balearics (Majorca, Minorca, Ibiza, Formentera, and Cabrera) and the seven Canaries (Tenerife, La Palma, Gomera, Hierro, Gran Canaria, Fuerteventura, and Lanzarote).

The Balearics lie in the Mediterranean off the eastern coast of Spain, about 15 miles (24 km) east of Valencia. They are famous for their beaches, spectacular cliffs, and rocky coves. There are 769 miles (1,240 km) of coastline in all which have made them a popular tourist attraction. Majorca is the largest island at 1,405 square miles (3,639 sq km), while Formentera is just 50 square miles (80 sq km). Besides the coastline, the islands have fine mountain scenery, inland plains used for farming, and a great diversity of wildlife, including many rare birds.

The Canary Islands lie far to the southwest of Spain, 713 miles (1,150 km) away in the north Atlantic. These islands are of volcanic origin.

CLIMATE AND WEATHER

The most extreme climate in Spain is in the capital, Madrid. Because it is right in the center of the land mass of the Iberian Peninsula and on the top of a high plateau, Madrid suffers from very hot summers and freezing winters. It gets so hot in August that the city of San Sebastian on Spain's cooler north coast becomes the government seat.

In summer, Madrid's temperature soars to more than 104°F (40°C). In winter it drops to -4°F (-20°C).

The northern coast has cold winters and warm, humid summers. Misty rain can cover the region for days on end, so the area is very green. Unfortunately, it also often has a gray smog around it because of pollution from the coal and iron centers there. To the

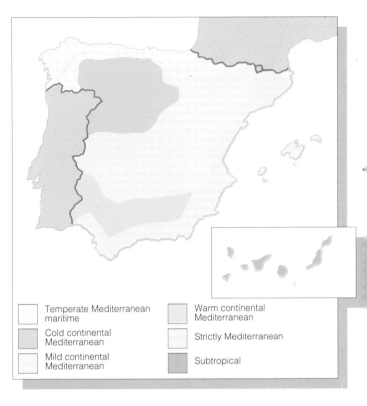

	Temperate Mediterranean maritime		Warm continental Mediterranean
	Cold continental Mediterranean		Strictly Mediterranean
	Mild continental Mediterranean		Subtropical

KEY FACTS

● The Sierra Nevada mountains in the south of Spain are covered by snow for 200 days each year at the summit.

● In the Canaries rain falls only during the winter months, and the total for the year averages only 8–12 inches (200–300 mm) in most places.

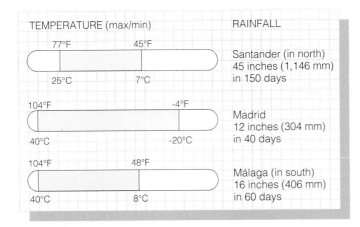

TEMPERATURE (max/min)		RAINFALL

| 77°F | 45°F | Santander (in north) 45 inches (1,146 mm) in 150 days |
| 25°C | 7°C | |

| 104°F | -4°F | Madrid 12 inches (304 mm) in 40 days |
| 40°C | -20°C | |

| 104°F | 48°F | Málaga (in south) 16 inches (406 mm) in 60 days |
| 40°C | 8°C | |

◀ *In the north, it is cool and wet with a lot of rain in the winter and sometimes in the summer. In Madrid, winters are very cold but dry; there are few days of rain all year. In the south, winters are mild, and summers are hot and dry.*

east of this area is the Pyrenean region of Navarra and Aragon, where in areas above 985 feet (300 m) there are an average of 56 days of snowfall each year.

The Mediterranean coast of Spain and the Balearic Islands have what most people imagine is the typical Spanish climate — hot, sunny summers and mild winters. In the south, the Sierra Nevada mountains are covered with snow, and in the winter it is often possible to sunbathe on the beaches of the Costa del Sol in the morning and drive up to the mountains to ski in the afternoon.

The Canary Islands are as far south as the Sahara Desert, but the GULF STREAM brings them cool breezes. Even in winter the islands have a warm, dry climate with temperatures of up to 64°F (18°C).

◀ *Because summer sun is almost guaranteed, Spain has become one of the most popular places in Europe for vacations. It can get rather overcrowded!*

▶ *In the Sierra Nevada mountains in southern Spain there is snow most winters, but there is often warm, sunny weather on the ski slopes.*

The aqueduct in Segovia, built by the Romans, is still used today. It brings water to the city from the Frio River 4 miles (6 km) away.

One of the few places in Spain where hydro-electric power has been harnessed is here in Alcántara, with the dam over the Tagus River.

Spain has very few natural resources, such as fossil fuels or minerals. Those it does have, such as coalfields and iron ore deposits, are mainly found in the north, where communication with the rest of the country is poor. These older industries are becoming increasingly unproductive. Most raw materials are imported, including oil.

Because much of the country is mountainous, Spain has always had a problem with internal transportation (roads, railroads, and canals). Parts of the country are also very dry, and there are very few navigable rivers. Water supply is another problem. After the civil war (1936–1939) and the period of economic expansion that followed, Spain suffered from severe deforestation. Since the death of General Franco in 1975, there has been a program of planting trees, and Spain now has the biggest area of forest and woodland — more than 37 million acres (15 million ha) — of any country in Europe.

Spain depends on imported petroleum

products for 68 percent of all the energy it uses — much more than any other European country. It has also developed nuclear energy and is planning to increase its hydroelectric power as well as other energy sources, such as wind power.

The country's most valuable natural resource is its climate. It is ideal for all kinds of farming, making Spain one of the largest exporters of food in Europe, supplying grains, citrus and other fruits, olives, vegetables, and grapes for its famous wines and sherries.

►*Barcelona is one of Spain's principal ports. Many of the country's vital energy imports (e.g., oil) arrive by sea. Exports of food, wine, and other bulky products go by ship, too.*

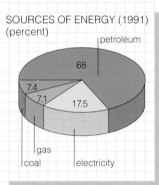

SOURCES OF ENERGY (1991)
(percent)

petroleum
68
7.4
7.1
17.5
gas
coal
electricity

◄*Spain is highly dependent on imported petroleum for its energy supplies. Its own natural resources of oil and coal are very small.*

▼*Spain has the largest area of forested land of any country in Europe.*

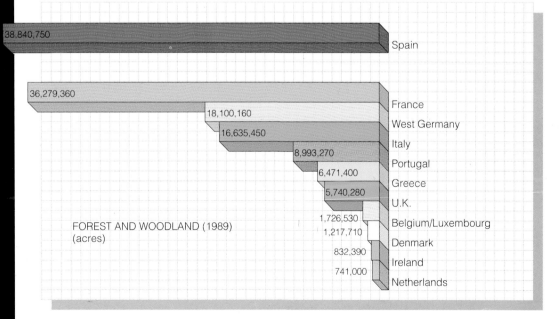

FOREST AND WOODLAND (1989)
(acres)

38,840,750	Spain
36,279,360	France
18,100,160	West Germany
16,635,450	Italy
8,993,270	Portugal
6,471,400	Greece
5,740,280	U.K.
1,726,530	Belgium/Luxembourg
1,217,710	Denmark
832,390	Ireland
741,000	Netherlands

Castilian, the language of central Spain, is what most of us think of as Spanish. But there are several other languages in the various regions, as well as many other cultural differences between places.

REGIONAL DIFFERENCES

The best known of these regional languages is Basque, which is different from any other language in the world. No one knows its origins, though it is believed to be very ancient and may have been the language of the original inhabitants of the Iberian Peninsula.

Many Basque people work in the numerous factories and mines in the region. Other Basques live more traditional lives, such as the farmers who move their herds of sheep, goats, and cows into the mountains in spring and down to the valleys in winter.

▲*Flamenco dancing, known as Sevillana in Spain, is very popular in the south of the country. Most children also learn it to dance at fiestas.*

▶ *Pelota is a very fast Basque ball game. It is played in a court, rather like squash. It used to be played outdoors, using the walls of houses in the village square as the court. You have to be physically fit to play pelota.*

Barcelona is the main city of Catalonia and the capital of the Catalan language, which appears on road signs in this region together with Castilian Spanish. Catalonia also has television and radio stations that broadcast in Catalan.

Other areas with their own languages include Galicia in the northwest, where Galician is a mixture of Spanish and Portuguese. The Galicians enjoy their own rather Scottish-sounding music, playing bagpipes and dancing jigs. Around Valencia in eastern Spain, Catalan is mixed with Spanish, while in Majorca in the Balearic Islands there is a strong French influence on the language.

ANDALUSIA

There are other regional differences besides language. Andalusia, for instance, is the traditional home of flamenco dancing, though now this can be seen and heard all over Spain. It is thought to have been brought by the MOORS, who invaded Spain from North Africa in A.D. 711. They governed in the south for almost 800 years, and their influence can be seen most strongly in Andalusia.

Houses in Andalusia still have the Moorish thick walls and few windows, to keep out the fierce sun. They were often built around a shady courtyard, where people would sit even on the hottest day and might be cooled further by a fountain. The Moors carved stone as delicately as lace and made beautiful ceramic tiles with intricate and colorful patterns. Many of their picturesque buildings survive in Andalusia, and among the most famous are the Alhambra ("red castle") Palace in Granada, the Giralda Tower in Seville, and Cordoba's mosque. The Moors introduced new foods,

KEY FACTS

● When General Franco ruled Spain (1939–1975), the only language allowed to be spoken there was Castilian.
● One out of every four Spaniards speaks another language besides Spanish.
● The Moors left their mark in the food and the language of Spain. For instance, they introduced the orange – *naranj* in Arabic, *naranja* in Spanish (which eventually became "an orange" in English).
● Because the Moors were Moslems, their religion forbade them to draw people, so Moorish craftsmen made intricate patterned carvings instead.
● In the 1930s, 75% of Spain's population lived in the countryside. Today the figure is just 16%.

▼ *In many areas of Spain there are local dialects and even quite different languages, the most famous of which is Basque.*

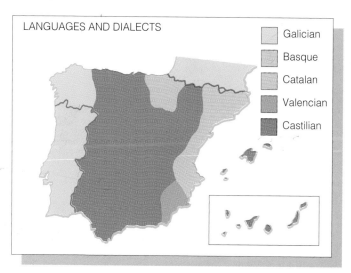

LANGUAGES AND DIALECTS

- Galician
- Basque
- Catalan
- Valencian
- Castilian

too, such as oranges, rice, and sugarcane, which had never been grown before in Europe.

THE COUNTRYSIDE

Although each of Spain's regions has a strong identity of its own, changes in the country's economy mean that many people are leaving the countryside to find work in the big cities and in the tourist industry. Madrid and Barcelona are the principal cities where new industries, such as movies and fashion, are flourishing. Tourism is also thriving on the Spanish islands and along the coast.

This means that large areas of the country are emptying, with 47% of the population now living on just 15% of the land. Most of the people who are leaving are young working people. This means that much of the countryside is now inhabited by a growing majority of older people. This in turn is causing local economies to decline because they have a smaller work force available. In the meantime, a growing proportion of the population is living in a smaller area, with cities and tourist centers sprawling outward in urban developments.

This trend can be seen in the figures for population density in Spain. The average figure for the country is 202 people per square mile (77 people per sq km), but there are wide variations. Madrid has 1,580 per square mile (607 per sq km) and there are 530 per square mile (203 per sq km) in the tourist areas of the Canary Islands, while in Castile in the center of the country the figure is only 65 per square mile (25 per sq km).

◄ *In Barcelona, the capital of Catalonia, the road signs are written in Catalan, the local language, as well as Castilian Spanish.*

► *The Alhambra Palace in Granada was built by the Moors. Their beautiful stonework, so delicate it looks like lace, is seen here in the Lions' Court.*

The family is at the heart of daily life in Spain. Outings of big family groups — mothers, fathers, children, aunts, uncles, cousins, and grandparents — are very common. Because families tend to do everything together, babysitters are almost unknown in Spain. Even if it means staying up late and going to a restaurant at night, children tend to be included in whatever is happening.

THE EFFECT OF THE CLIMATE

The hot summers give a special timetable to the day. During the middle of the day, it is too hot to work, and in the early evening most people find it too hot to eat. Breakfast is normally very light — toast or a croissant with coffee. Almost everyone in Spain makes up for this with a *bocadillo* (a crusty

▲*Eating out is a popular Spanish pastime. Because of the warm weather, restaurants usually have tables outside.*

▼*Spanish people usually have two surnames: the first is the father's, the second is the mother's. When a woman marries, she may keep her own name, or drop her mother's name and add her husband's. So María Díaz Servet would become María Díaz de Ortíz. As a couple they would be known as Los Señores de Ortíz.*

HOW SPANISH NAMES WORK		
FATHER Juan Velazquez Ortíz	}	**SON** Mañuel Velazquez Díaz
MOTHER María Díaz Servet		

roll with cheese or ham) in the middle of the morning. People who work in shops and offices usually go out to the local café or bar for their *bocadillo*.

Lunch does not start until 2 or 2:30 P.M. It is often the main meal of the day and can last to the middle of the afternoon. In some places, people take a SIESTA, or afternoon nap, afterward. Children sometimes have a little snack, but dinner is not until 9:30 or 10 P.M., or even later on weekends. Before dinner on warm summer evenings, people visit TAPAS bars where little snacks, such as olives, anchovies, octopus, or slices of tortilla (Spanish omelette) are served with drinks. Or they simply stroll around looking in store windows and greeting friends and neighbors during the nightly PASEO or walk around the main streets and squares.

Because of the long break in the middle of the day, school and work both continue until later in the day than they do in cooler countries. Because it is too hot to go to

KEY FACTS

● All religions except Roman Catholicism were outlawed in Spain in the late 15th century. Today there are still only 30,000 Protestants, 12,000 Jews and 1,000 Moslems in the country.

● The biggest cathedral in the world is Santa Maria in Seville – 126 metres long and 82 metres wide. It was built between 1402 and 1506.

● People in Spain are increasingly likely to live in cities rather than rural areas – two-fifths of the population now live in towns with more than 10,000 inhabitants.

● Football is the most popular sport in Spain, followed by bull-fighting. Both are shown regularly on TV.

school in summer, the school vacation lasts from the end of June to the middle of September.

EDUCATION

Compulsory state education begins when children are 6 years old, but many start nursery schools as young as 2 years old. There are frequent school examinations. At

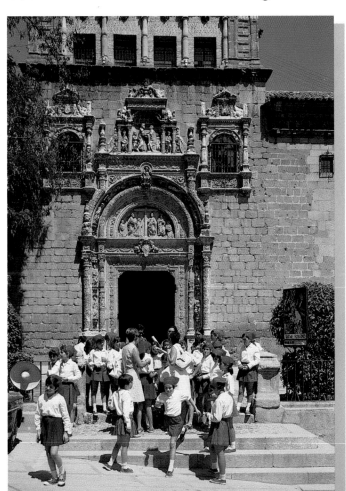

◀ *Schoolchildren, seen here in Toledo, start the day early and finish late. But they have a long midday break, as it is too hot to work then.*

DAILY SCHEDULE	
7 A.M.	Breakfast
8:30–9 A.M.	School/work
2 P.M.	Lunch/siesta
4–6 P.M.	School
4–7 P.M.	Work
4–8 P.M.	Shops open again
7–9 P.M.	Paseo
9–11 P.M.	Dinner

the age of 16, the academically minded who pass the BACHILLERATO (equivalent to SATs) can go on to a pre-university course. However, many go instead to a job training program, where they work some of the week and go to college the rest of the time.

RELIGION

Religion is very important in Spain, and most Spaniards are Roman Catholics. Spanish churches are often quite big and elaborately decorated, even in the smallest villages. All the churches have statues of Jesus, Mary, and the saints, and these are taken out and carried on floats through the streets on special days. One of the most famous of these processions takes place in Seville during Easter week, known in Spain as *Semana Santa* (Holy Week). It begins on Palm Sunday and continues until Good Friday. Some floats show scenes from the story of Jesus' life. Many are lit with candles, and each float is carried on the shoulders of approximately 50 men, who walk barefoot through the streets. They

▲*The population of Spanish cities has grown rapidly in recent years and the cities have had to expand in order to accommodate the people arriving from the countryside. Most city dwellers live in big apartment buildings.*

◄*In Las Ramblas in Barcelona, as in every Spanish town, people take an early evening stroll, or paseo, before dinner.*

NATIONAL FIESTAS (HOLIDAYS)

New Year's Day	El día del Año Nuevo
Epiphany	Los Reyes Magos (January 6)
Victory Day	El día de Victoria (March 1)
Saint Joseph's Day	El día de San José (March 19)
Holy Week	Semana Santa
Good Friday	Viernes Santo
Easter	Pascua
Ascension Day	La Ascensión
Whitsun	El Pentecostes
Corpus Christi	El Corpus
Saint James	El día de Santiago (July 25)
Assumption	La Asunción (August 15)
Virgin of Pilar	El día de Virgen del Pilar (October 12)
All Saints' Day	El día de todos los Santos (November 1)
Immaculate Conception and Mothers' Day	La Concepción (December 8)
Christmas Day	El día de Navidad

wear long robes and tall, pointed hats with slits to see through. It is considered to be a great honor to help carry a float.

Christmas is another important FIESTA (festival) in Spain, but it is mainly a time for religious and family celebrations. Spanish children have to wait until Epiphany (January 6) to get their presents. This is known as the day of the three kings, and many towns celebrate it with sweets thrown to the children from floats. In Majorca, men dressed as the kings arrive by sea and distribute presents on the shore.

There are many other religious holidays

▶ ***Most Spaniards are Roman Catholics and religious festivals are taken very seriously. In this Easter procession, men known as "penitents" carry a statue of the Virgin Mary through the streets.***

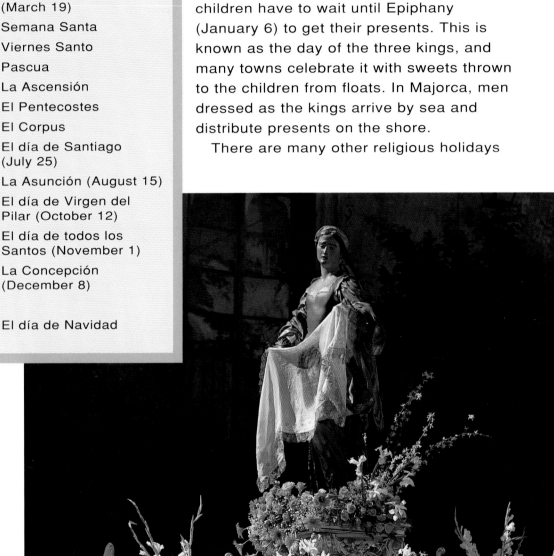

In rural Spain, life seems to have remained the same for centuries, with spotless whitewashed houses, mules for transportation, and conversations with neighbors. Yet this village is near Málaga, one of the main resorts on the Costa del Sol.

throughout the year, all celebrated by fiestas that take different forms in different parts of the country. They always include an enormous street, or town, party, with lots of singing, dancing, and regional costumes. Every town has its own patron saint, and saints' days are popular occasions for celebrations. In Madrid, the patron saint is San Isidro. Around this saint's day in May, there are huge parties with lots of events,

such as bullfighting, soccer games, concerts, plays, and folk dancing. The celebrations last 10 or 11 days. At the San Fermín fiesta in Pamplona in northern Spain in July, young men run through the streets with bulls chasing after them. At the Fallas fiesta in Valencia during March, enormous papier-mâché floats can be seen on the streets. On the last night they are all set alight at the same time as a spectacular fireworks display.

BULLFIGHTING

Although there are some Spaniards who object to it, bullfighting is still a very popular sport in Spain. It is said to have begun in pre-Roman times. Today it is watched not only in bullrings, but on television, too.

In Spain, bullfights are called corridas and usually take place late on Sunday afternoons during the season, which lasts from spring until autumn. Because it is very hot, the expensive seats are the ones in the shade (*sombra*), while the cheap seats are in the sun (*sol*). They start with a parade of

KEY FACTS

● The bull-ring in Madrid holds 23,000 spectators.
● Real Madrid have won the European Cup 6 times. ("Real" means "royal").
● Spain has 77 golf courses, including Europe's only flood-lit golf course at Marbella.

toreros (bullfighters). Picadors fight on horseback, but the star of the show is the MATADOR with his black, three-cornered hat, embroidered cape, and "suit of lights" — a short satin jacket and tight breeches decorated in silver and gold.

The bull is provoked and weakened by the lances of the picadors, and the matador goes through a series of elaborate "passes" until he has won control over the bull. Then he kills it by plunging his sword between the bull's horns. If the crowd thinks the matador is brave and skillful, there is great applause and cheering. If not, he can be booed and jeered out of the ring.

▲ *This poster is advertising a bullfight.*

▶ *Although bullfighting is regarded as cruel in many countries, in Spain it is generally seen as both the national sport and an art requiring great skill.*

RULES AND LAWS

Parts of Spain, particularly the south, were ruled by the Moors from North Africa for nearly 800 years. The Moors were very tolerant; they were Muslims, but they did not force other people to adopt their religion. Christians and Jews were allowed freedom of worship. Religious persecution did not begin until the reign of King Ferdinand and Queen Isabella in the late 15th century, when the Moors and Jews were driven out.

Ferdinand and Isabella also sponsored Christopher Columbus' exploration of the New World. As a result, Spain became very rich and powerful. Its empire included most of Central and South America. Spanish is still the third most widely spoken language in the world today, after Mandarin Chinese and English.

Earlier this century, Spain was isolated from the rest of the world. In 1936 a civil war broke out, which was won in 1939 by General Franco. He established a harsh dictatorship, which survived until his death in 1975. Franco had declared that he would revive the monarchy, and after he died, King Juan Carlos came to the throne. The first free elections for 40 years were held in 1977, and Spain joined the European Community and NATO in 1986.

Spain is now a DEMOCRACY. After a general election, the monarch asks the leader of the winning party to form a government. The country is divided into 14 regions, each with its own elected parliament and administration funded by the central government. Each region has its own capital and flag. The Basques have their own police force, too. The central parliament is called the Cortes. It has 554

▲ *King Juan Carlos and Queen Sofía are very popular with Spaniards. The monarchy is regarded as a protection for democracy after the years of dictatorship.*

▼ *Spain is a democratic monarchy. The Cortes (national parliament) is made up of the Congreso and the Senado. Each of the 14 regions has its own local parliament, too.*

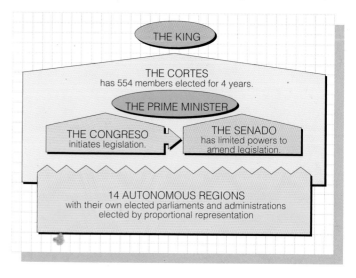

THE KING

THE CORTES
has 554 members elected for 4 years.

THE PRIME MINISTER

THE CONGRESO initiates legislation.	THE SENADO has limited powers to amend legislation.

14 AUTONOMOUS REGIONS
with their own elected parliaments and administrations
elected by proportional representation

members and is elected for four years.

Since the death of General Franco, changes have taken place very rapidly in Spain. There have been new laws to protect people's rights at work. Divorce is now permitted, and a WELFARE STATE is being established. Most people welcome these changes, but there is a large minority, mainly among older people, who feel that everything is happening too quickly and that Spain is moving too far from the teachings of the church.

There are three central police forces in Spain: the Policía Armada, who carry guns and guard official buildings; the Guardias Civiles, who are also armed and patrol in cars or on motorcycles; and the Urbanos, who are the traffic police.

Spain's great empire did not last long, but the Spanish language is still used in many countries throughout the world.

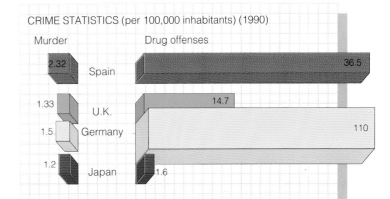

CRIME STATISTICS (per 100,000 inhabitants) (1990)

	Murder	Drug offenses
Spain	2.32	36.5
U.K.	1.33	14.7
Germany	1.5	110
Japan	1.2	1.6

Drug offenses have recently become a problem among young people in the big cities.

The Guardias Civiles, who carry guns, are the main police force in Spain.

KEY FACTS

● Madrid was made the capital of the country in 1561 because it was right in the center of the country. There was nothing there before, except the remains of a Moorish fortress.

● Many of the Basque people in northern Spain want their own independent state. ETA, the Basque separatist group, was established in 1959.

● In 1981 a group of army officers attempted to take over the country, but their leaders surrendered to the king.

● Three hundred million people in 21 countries speak Spanish as their first language. Another 24 million in the U.S. also speak Spanish as their first language.

FOOD AND FARMING

Spain has many varied kinds of agriculture because of its great diversity of land and climate. In the mountains of the north, there are pastures for cows, sheep, and goats. The plains of the meseta in central Spain grow arable crops. The warm Mediterranean and southern regions grow fruits and vegetables, such as grapes and olives. More exotic produce, like avocado pears, bananas, and papaya fruit, grow in the subtropical climate of the Canary Islands.

Although farming methods are becoming more up-to-date in Spain, in many areas people still farm in the traditional way. In December, for instance, the olive harvest is picked by hand, often by whole families

▼ *Because of its climate, Spain is able to grow and export food and wine all over the world. Much of it goes to its EC neighbors.*

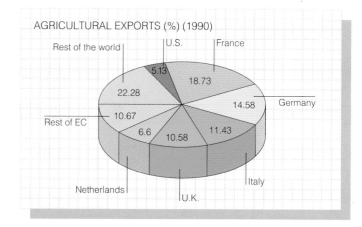

AGRICULTURAL EXPORTS (%) (1990)

Rest of the world — 22.28
U.S. — 5.13
France — 18.73
Germany — 14.58
Italy — 11.43
U.K. — 10.58
Netherlands — 6.6
Rest of EC — 10.67

working together. The green olives have to be picked very carefully so that they do not get bruised. Most are left on the trees to turn black and are then knocked down by people using sticks so the olives can be picked up from the ground. Then they are pressed to make olive oil.

Grapes are another important Spanish crop. With France and Italy, Spain is one of the largest wine producers in the world. Spain bottles 3 million tons a year, compared with 7 million in Italy and 6.5 million in France, from its 57 grape-growing regions. The most famous of Spain's many different wines is rioja. Spanish champagne is known as "cava." Sherry comes from the region around the area of Jerez, and its

KEY FACTS

● The Spanish eat more fish and less sugar than any other Europeans – an average of 38 kilos of fish and 24 kilos of sugar per person each year (compared with 19 kilos of fish and 40 kilos of sugar in Britain).

● In 1990 the total Spanish fishing catch was over 974,000 tonnes, including 141,000 tonnes of molluscs (eg squid) and crustaceans (eg lobster).

● Oranges grow on the trees of the towns of the south as decoration. The Spaniards find these Seville oranges too bitter to eat, but some are exported.

● Britain takes 65% of Spain's exported bitter oranges, using them to make marmalade.

● Olive trees live for centuries on the dry hillsides of Spain.

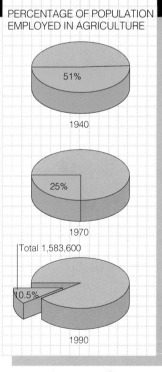

PERCENTAGE OF POPULATION EMPLOYED IN AGRICULTURE

51%
1940

25%
1970

Total 1,583,600
10.5%
1990

◀ *Paella is a Spanish dish of saffron-colored rice with meat, fish, and seafood – though it is not usually made on such a large scale as this!*

▲ *The hams, sausages, and cheeses of Spain are famous, and every region has its own specialty. This picture shows a butcher's stand in Barcelona.*

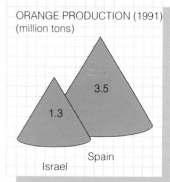

ORANGE PRODUCTION (1991)
(million tons)

1.3 Israel

3.5 Spain

▲ **Spain produces more than twice as many oranges as Israel, its main competitor.**
◄ **In Andalusia, oranges are picked by hand.**

► **Spain grows many nuts as well as fruits. These almond trees blossom in the early spring.**

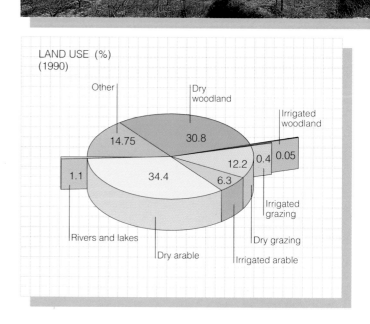

English name was originally an attempt to pronounce "Jerez." Sherry is kept in casks in cool warehouses, called bodegas, before it is bottled, and many tourists visit the bodegas to sample the sherry.

Farming has become much more mechanized and intensive in Mediterranean Spain. There has been a lot of investment, and Spain has received considerable aid from the EC to improve its farming and fishing, which are very important to the Spanish economy. Increasing mechanization has meant that fewer people work on the land now. In 1960, the figure was 5 million people, but now just 1.5 million are involved in farming.

Spain is famous for its hams (*jamon*) and sausages (*chorizos*). There are many different regional cheeses, too, often made

LAND USE (%)
(1990)

Other 14.75

Dry woodland 30.8

Irrigated woodland 0.05

Irrigated grazing 0.4

Dry grazing 12.2

Irrigated arable 6.3

Dry arable 34.4

Rivers and lakes 1.1

from goats' milk, such as a hard white cheese from La Mancha, which is called *Manchego*. Spanish people also eat a lot of fish and shellfish. One of the most famous Spanish dishes is paella, which is eaten all over Spain but comes originally from Valencia, the main rice-growing area of Spain. Paella is a mixture of rice, shellfish, little pieces of chicken and meat, red peppers, and black olives. It is cooked and served in a big dish called a paella, and it is traditionally made over an open fire.

Fish is very popular in the north, too, and there are many fishing villages along the coast. Shellfish, cod, and baby eels are caught there. Much of the catch is taken overnight in trucks to Madrid.

In the south, Andalusia is the home of deep fried food and gazpacho, a refreshing cold soup made from tomatoes, peppers, and cucumbers. *Alioli*, a garlic-flavored mayonnaise, was created in Catalonia. And mayonnaise itself comes from Mahón in Minorca.

Although the Spanish eat a great deal of meat, especially lamb, veal, pork, and kid goat, they have also invented many

vegetarian dishes and eat many pulses (peas, beans, and lentils). A famous dish from Asturias in the north of Spain is *fabada*, made from white beans.

Spain is hard to beat in its variety of fruits and vegetables. Oranges, lettuce, onions, carrots, spinach, and much more produce are available, all very fresh and very cheap. Most Spaniards buy their produce in the local market. Most towns have a market every day, with a permanent building for stands. Even tiny villages usually have a weekly street market. Many people prefer to shop there and take the opportunity to talk with their neighbors at the same time.

▼ *Fishing is an important industry for the coastal villages of northern Spain. Here fishermen unload the sardine catch.*

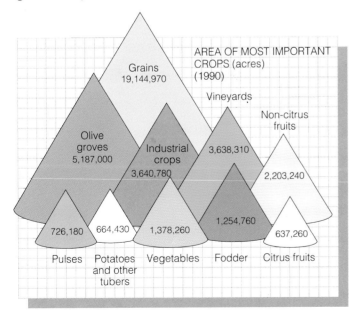

AREA OF MOST IMPORTANT CROPS (acres) (1990)

Grains 19,144,970

Vineyards

Non-citrus fruits

Olive groves 5,187,000

Industrial crops 3,640,780

3,638,310

2,203,240

726,180

664,430

1,378,260

1,254,760

637,260

Pulses

Potatoes and other tubers

Vegetables

Fodder

Citrus fruits

TRADE AND INDUSTRY

Coal, iron, and steel industries, including shipbuilding, which used to be important industries for Spain, have declined in the last two decades. But newer manufacturing industries have been set up, such as electronics, chemicals, computers, and car production. However, because of its isolation during General Franco's dictatorship, Spain still lags behind more technologically advanced countries.

Some traditional businesses have adapted more quickly. For instance, the clothing, leather, and footwear industry has developed new fashion houses in Madrid and Barcelona. Movies are also important. Spain has a flourishing film industry, and in 1991 its output of 64 movies was the fourth highest in Europe, after France (156), Italy (129), and Germany (72).

▲ *Spanish sherry is famous all over the world, but it is particularly loved by the British, who have been importing it since the 16th century.*

KEY FACTS

● More people visit Spain each year than any other country.
● In the tourist areas, incomes are on average 20% higher than in industrial districts.
● The Spanish car industry has grown considerably over recent years. By 1988, Spain was the fourth largest car producer in Europe.
● Spain has one of the highest levels of female unemployment in Europe. The European average of unemployed women is 12%. In Spain it is 25.3%.

One of the most important sectors of the Spanish economy is tourism. There are now approximately 52 million tourists a year — 14 million more than Spain's entire population. The building and service industries are thriving as people create and run hotels, restaurants, stores, and whole new towns built especially for tourists.

Tourism has affected other Spanish industries, too. Airports have had to expand because more than 37 million foreign visitors pass through a Spanish airport every year. Craft industries have also become big business, particularly leather and the colorful ceramics for which Spain is famous.

Spain's wine and sherry businesses are important, too. Its sherry is exported to 120 countries around the world.

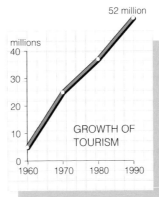

GROWTH OF TOURISM

52 million

millions

GROSS DOMESTIC PRODUCT (%) (1991)

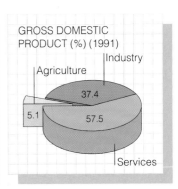

Agriculture — 5.1
Industry — 37.4
Services — 57.5

▲ *Traditional crafts, such as lace-making, are thriving again because of the tourist industry. Many visitors like to take home a souvenir of Spain.*

▼ *Another flourishing craft is pottery. Spanish ceramics are popular because of their bright colors, seen here on display outside a Majorcan shop.*

PRODUCTION AND EXPORT OF SPANISH CARS

Production	Exports	
1,402,572	706,705	1987
1,477,367	787,089	1988
1,637,776	925,349	1989
1,679,301	1,066,007	1990
1,773,675	1,284,447	1991

Spain has had to make big changes in its communications network over the last 20 years. New roads are being built or widened all the time to cope with the huge increase in traffic. Around 90 percent of people traveling in Spain go by road, and 75 percent of all goods are transported by road, too. This has caused particular problems in the cities and along the coast in summer, when the resorts are full. The air is polluted, and the streets are often jammed with cars, trucks, and buses.

Trunk, or main, roads (*carreteras*) usually have just one lane for traffic. On most highways (*autopistas*) drivers have to pay a toll, although this is not usually very expensive. Speed limits in Spain allow drivers on highways to travel at up to 80 miles an hour (130 km an hour).

The tracks on Spanish railroad lines are wider apart than those in most European countries, except for Portugal. They were built 9 inches (233 mm) wider to take the more powerful trains that were needed to cope with Spain's mountainous countryside. However, the new Talgo train has been built with the capability of changing from Spanish tracks to those used elsewhere in Europe. High-speed trains are also being introduced to Spain now, and these can cut

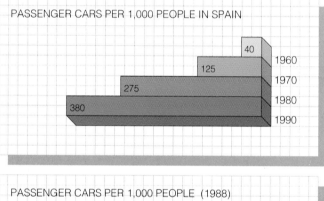

PASSENGER CARS PER 1,000 PEOPLE IN SPAIN

40	1960
125	1970
275	1980
380	1990

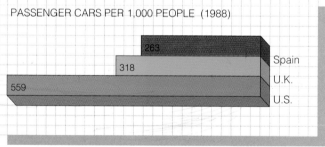

PASSENGER CARS PER 1,000 PEOPLE (1988)

263	Spain
318	U.K.
559	U.S.

◀ *Although Spain is receiving many grants from the EC to develop transportation and communications as a priority, in rural areas the mule is still the most convenient means of transportation, taking produce from the fields to the market.*

the 334-mile (538-km) journey from Madrid in the center to Seville in the south, from 6.25 hours to just 2.5 hours.

The fastest growing form of transportation in Spain is air travel, as millions of foreign tourists arrive each year. Charter flights began in the 1960s, and by 1990, nearly 25 million charter passengers were arriving in Spanish airports on their way to their vacations in the sun. In all, more than 70 million passengers travel through Spanish airports every year. Nearly 38 million of them are on international flights.

KEY FACTS

● Only the new Talgo train can cross the border into France because it can change from the wider Spanish lines to the narrower ones used in the rest of Europe.
● Spain has no canals and very few rivers, so there has never been any internal navigation in the country.
● Spain now has 15 million vehicles on the road, 80% of which are passenger cars, and a total road length of 200,880 miles (324,000 km).

▶ *El Tren Ave ("The Bird Train") takes just 2.5 hours to travel the 334 miles (538 km) from Madrid to Seville.*

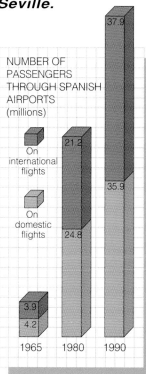

NUMBER OF PASSENGERS THROUGH SPANISH AIRPORTS (millions)

On international flights

On domestic flights

37.9

21.2

35.9

24.8

3.9
4.2

1965   1980   1990

THE ENVIRONMENT

From the 1960s, Spain was developed very rapidly. There were no controls over the apartments and tourist hotels that were built along the coast, and a long urban sprawl replaced a shoreline of spectacular natural beauty. During this period of economic growth, new industries were developed, too, and there were no controls over pollution of the air, water, or land. A great deal of damage was done. Spain has only recently become aware of the importance of caring for its natural environment.

Besides the problems created by people, Spain's climate has caused other problems. The dry conditions in the south have meant that forest fires and desertification of the land, as it becomes drier and unable to support any vegetation, have become common.

However, Spain's environmental problems are mainly in its cities and tourist developments. There are still vast areas of countryside with few people and no pollution. There are also nine national parks where unusual animals, birds, and plants flourish.

The most famous national park in the country is the Doñana, on the southeastern coast, near Huelva, close to the border with Portugal. It is the largest national park in Europe, covering 293 square miles (758 km²). Thousands of birds spend the winter here on the salt marshes — from geese escaping the cold northern European winters, to exotic flamingoes. It is also the home of some species that are not found in any other country, such as the imperial eagle, Egyptian mongoose, and Iberian lynx.

The mountain national parks in northern Spain are in complete contrast. These are high, thickly forested regions with beautiful lakes, where the weather is usually cool and damp. Many rare animals and birds live in these remote parts, including chamois, bears, wildcats, wolves, ptarmigan, and

◀ *La Mancha in central Spain has been famous for its wind power for centuries. It was here that Don Quixote, in Cervantes' book, "tilted at windmills."*

KEY FACTS

● Pollution from cars in Spain is growing, but at 228 tons of CO_2 emissions annually it is still well behind the U.S. at 5,974 tons.
● There has been little work in Spain on how to harness solar energy, even though there is plenty of sunshine there.

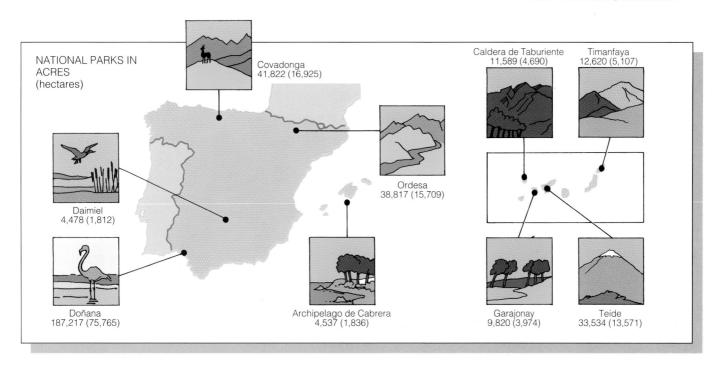

NATIONAL PARKS IN
ACRES
(hectares)

Covadonga
41,822 (16,925)

Ordesa
38,817 (15,709)

Daimiel
4,478 (1,812)

Doñana
187,217 (75,765)

Archipelago de Cabrera
4,537 (1,836)

Caldera de Taburiente
11,589 (4,690)

Timanfaya
12,620 (5,107)

Garajonay
9,820 (3,974)

Teide
33,534 (13,571)

▲ *Spain's varied climate and geography give it the widest range of national parks in Europe.*

◀ *The Iberian lynx is unique to Spain.*
▼ *The imperial eagle is now in danger of extinction.*

golden eagles.

Finally, there are the national parks in the Canary Islands. These dry volcanic landscapes are full of rare and beautiful flowers and trees — the Canary pine, the Canary cedar, and unusual laurels, heathers, herbs, violets, and daisies. But there is little animal wildlife in the Canary Island parks, apart from birds and lizards.

THE FUTURE

Spain has seen enormous changes in the past 20 years. During the 1970s, after the end of General Franco's dictatorship, it had the fastest growing economy in Europe, though this has now slowed down. As Spain opened its doors to new ideas, there were changes for both better and worse. One of the worst problems was caused by the development of tourist centers along the southern and Mediterranean coasts, with widespread and uncontrolled building that many people feel has spoiled the coastline.

Spanish people now have many more consumer goods than they did in the past, and imports are growing all the time. One of the biggest imports is of foreign cars. In 1980, about 42,000 cars were imported. By 1990, this figure had risen to 400,000.

There have been important changes for women, too. Until recently, few Spanish women went to work. Instead they stayed at home and looked after their children. Today things are very different and families are

SPAIN'S CAR IMPORTS

400,000

200,000

100,000

42,000

0

1980   1990

▼ *Seville's EXPO '92 meant the creation of many new buildings, such as this futuristic EC Tower.*

KEY FACTS

● Antonio Gaudí, Spain's most famous modern architect, designed Barcelona's Cathedral of the Sagrada Familia ("sacred family") more than 100 years ago. Gaudí died before the cathedral was finished, and in the 1980s a project to complete it was begun.

● While Great Britain still retains Gibraltar, Spain has two enclaves in Morocco — Ceuta and Melilla, where Spanish and Arabic are spoken.

● Spain has a young, growing population. A quarter of its people are under 16 years old.

smaller than they used to be. Although Spain still has one of Europe's highest unemployment rates for women — 25 percent, compared with a European average of 12 percent — many more women go out to work now than 20 years ago.

The future of Gibraltar has been an area of dispute between the British and the

One of Spain's new businesses in the fashion and cosmetics field, Adolfo Dominguez has a growing international reputation.

Spanish since the 1700s. Gibraltar has been controlled by the British since 1704, and it is still a British Dependent Territory. The British and Spanish each have customs posts on either side of the border. Many people from the mainland go to Gibraltar to shop, as goods there are not taxed and so they are cheaper to buy. Spain regards Gibraltar as part of its territory and wants to make it officially a part of Spain. However, most people who live there want to remain British, or to become independent. Gibraltar has been a source of disputes for hundreds of years and, for the moment at least, it looks likely to continue that way.

Spain joined the EC and NATO in 1986 and has become an active member of the European Community. In 1992 the country played its part in international events as Barcelona hosted the Olympic Games, Seville held a world fair (EXPO '92), and Madrid became European City of Culture.

Democracy in Spain is becoming more and more accepted, and the monarchy is very popular. However, many older people feel that change has happened too quickly and they are worried that Spanish traditions are disappearing. Some even feel that the strict rules imposed by General Franco were better for the country, and in 1981 there was an attempted takeover by a group of army officers. The leaders surrendered to the king. But most young people welcome the freedom and changes that democracy has brought to the country.

▶ *Another piece of eye-catching space-age architecture is the Telecom Tower in Barcelona, pointing the way forward to Spain's increasing modernism.*

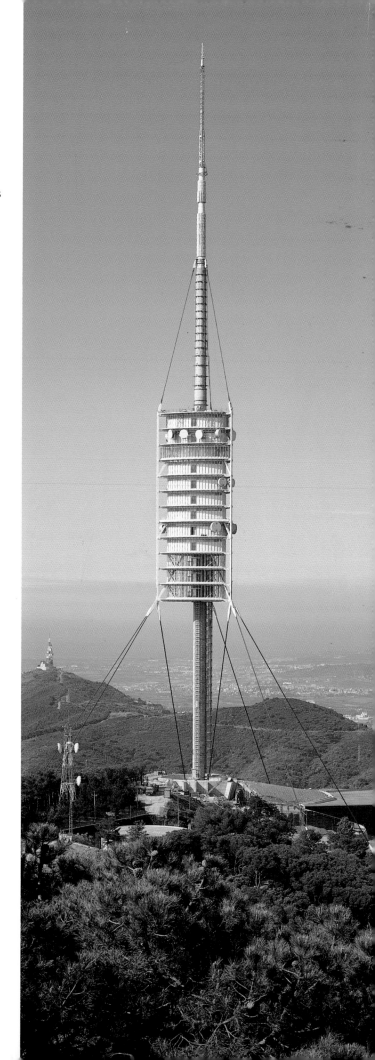

◀ *Even though Great Britain and Spain are both EC member countries, each still keeps guards on either side of Gibraltar's border.*

FURTHER INFORMATION

HISPANIC INSTITUTE
Columbia University, 612 W. 116th Street,
New York, NY 10027
HISPANIC SOCIETY OF AMERICA
613 West 155th Street, New York, NY 10032
IBERIA AIRLINES OF SPAIN
655 Madison Avenue, 20th floor, New York,
NY 10021
SPANISH EMBASSY
2700 15th Street N.W., Washington, D.C.
20009
SPANISH NATIONAL TOURISM OFFICE
665 5th Avenue, New York, NY 10022

BOOKS ABOUT SPAIN

Bailey, Donna. *Spain*. Raintree Steck-
Vaughn, 1992
Biggs, Betsey. *Kidding Around Spain: A
Young Person's Guide*. John Muir, 1991
Cummings, David. *Spain*. Watts, 1992
James, Ian. *Spain*. Watts, 1989
Loewen, Nancy. *Food in Spain*. Rourke,
1991
Shubert, Adrian. *The Land and People of
Spain*. HarperCollins Children's, 1992

GLOSSARY

BACHILLERATO
Spanish graduation examination, equivalent to SATs

DEFORESTATION
The large-scale destruction of forests, one of the causes of desertification.

DEMOCRACY
A country that is governed by the politicians elected by the people of that country

DESERTIFICATION
The deterioration of land into desert conditions. This is due to factors such as lack of rain, deforestation, and soil erosion, which make the land drier and drier until nothing will grow there.

DICTATORSHIP
A country governed by one person who has absolute power

FIESTA
Spanish word for a holiday or festival

GULF STREAM
A warm ocean current that flows from the Gulf of Mexico past northwest Africa and Western Europe

ISTHMUS
A narrow strip of land connecting two larger areas

MATADOR
The head bullfighter

MESETA
The central plateau of Spain. The word literally means "little table."

MOORS
People from North Africa who conquered Spain in A.D. 711 and controlled parts of it until 1492

PASEO
A nighttime stroll around town, window-shopping and meeting up with friends

PELOTA
A very fast Basque ball game

PLATEAU
A high flat plain

RIA
A rocky coastal inlet

SIERRA
Spanish word for mountains

SIESTA
Spanish word for an afternoon nap

TAPAS
Small portions of food served with drinks in Spanish cafés and bars

WELFARE STATE
A country where the government tries to look after the welfare of its people, providing free medical care and paying allowances such as pensions and unemployment benefits

INDEX

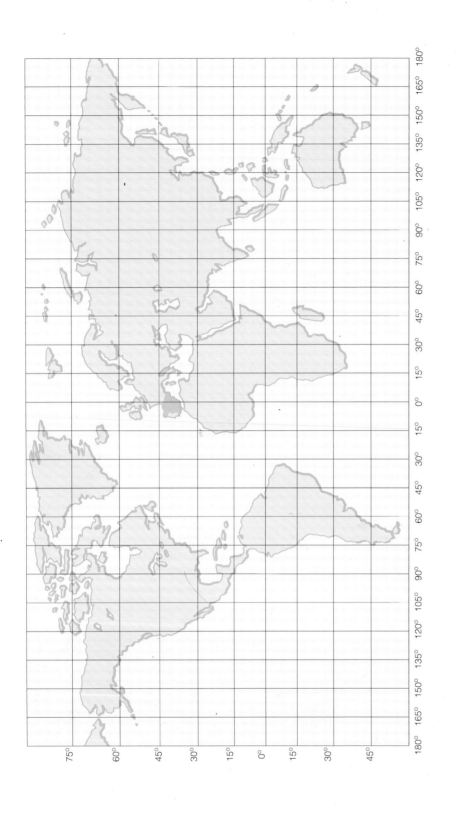

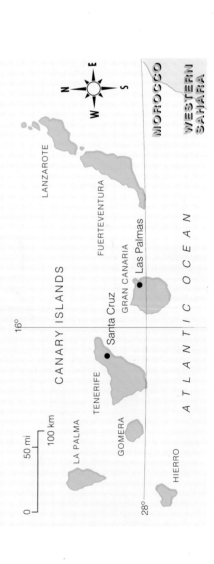

CANARY ISLANDS

LA PALMA

TENERIFE

GOMERA

HIERRO

Santa Cruz

LANZAROTE

FUERTEVENTURA

GRAN CANARIA

Las Palmas

MOROCCO

WESTERN SAHARA

A T L A N T I C   O C E A N

16°

28°

0

50 mi

100 km

N
W   E
S

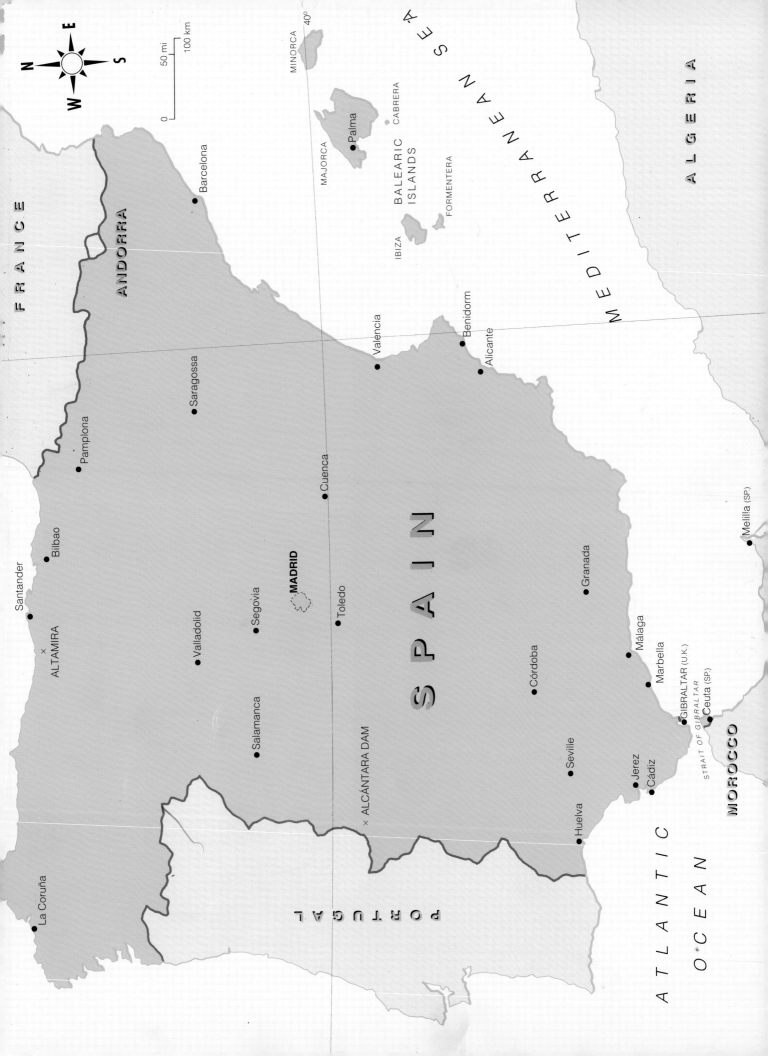